DARTMOOR COUN1

INCLUDING . . .
Ashburton, Haytor, Chagford, Okehampt᠊   ᠆ ᠆n,
Buckland Abbey, Dart Valley Railway, Buck᠊᠊᠊᠊. ᠊ovey, Postbridge,
Widecombe-in-the-Moor, Badger's Holt, Two Bridges, Princetown.

This guide book contains exact but simple directions for the motorist who wishes to combine visits to such well known places as Buckfast, Widecombe, Dartmeet, Princetown and Buckland Abbey, with an exploration of the quiet villages, woods and moorland that lie hidden beyond the more popular tourist routes.

The 'Main Circle' Route (Maps 1 – 10) shown on the Key Map opposite covers 120 miles, and mainly follows around the outer confines of Dartmoor. If from time to time we have had to lead you away from the moors we would excuse ourselves by claiming that there are occasionally no satisfactory alternatives. We have provided on Maps 3, 4 and 5, a route around Okehampton, but now that this town is by-passed by the busy A30, you may wish to visit Okehampton and re-join the main route at Map 5, Point L near Lydford, by using the A30 and the A386.

The 'Main Circle' Route is too long for a leisurely day's journey and you will note from the Key Map that we have included smaller (East and South) Circles. However if your time is limited we recommend the Special Moorland Route (Maps 1 – 2 – 11 – 12 – 13 – 14) which includes most of the more dramatic moorland roads within the space of 70 miles. It should also be stressed that each route being circular (apart from the Moorland Special), may be started and finished at any point suitable to you.

HOW TO USE YOUR BOOK ON THE ROUTE

Each double page makes up a complete picture of the country ahead of you. On the left you will find a one inch to the mile strip map, with the route marked by a series of dashes. Direction is always from top to bottom, so that the map may be looked at in conjunction with the 'directions to the driver', with which it is cross referenced by a letter itemising each junction point. This enables the driver to have exact guidance every time an opportunity for changing direction occurs, even if it is only 'Keep straight, not left!'

With mileage intervals shown, the driver should even have warning when to expect those 'moments of decision', and if a signpost exists we have used this to help you, with the 'Signposted' column. However re-signing is always in progress, and this may lead to slight differences in sign marking in some cases . . . So beware of freshly erected signs.

We have also included a description of the towns and villages through which you will pass, together with some photographs to illustrate the route.

To gain full enjoyment from your journeys, be prepared to leave your car as often as possible. Although much of Dartmoor's dark grandeur may be casually observed from a car, you will only capture its real magic if you are prepared to walk out and away from the inevitably busy roads and often crowded points of pilgrimage. Keep this in mind and Dartmoor will not disappoint you.

Compiled by PETER and HELEN TITCHMARSH
Revised by ALLAN and IRENE BLACKNALL
Photography by ALAN and PETER TITCHMARSH

Map 1  Directions / Sign-posted

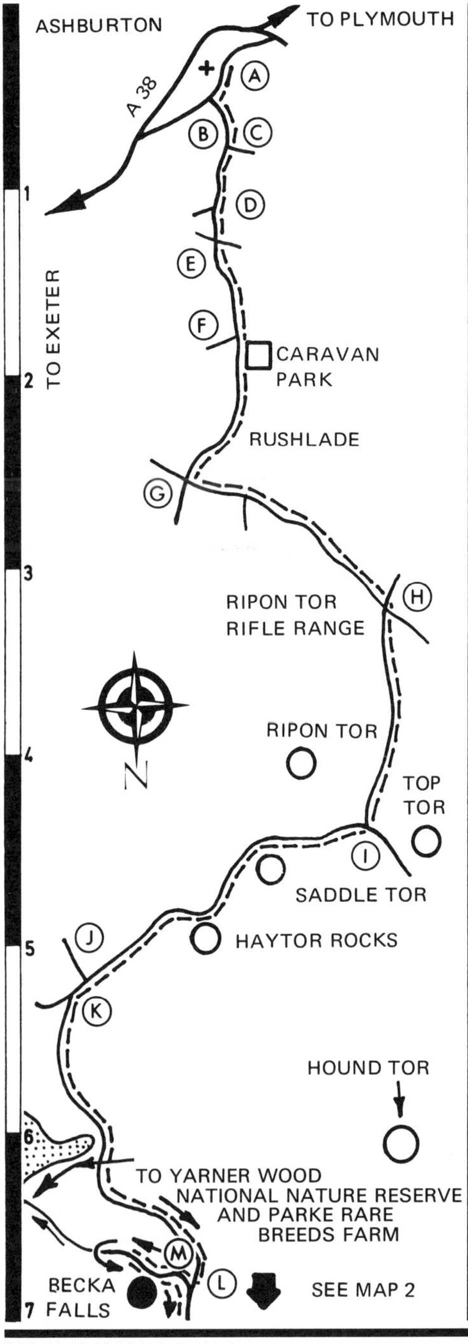

Ref.	kms / Miles	Directions	Sign-posted
A	0	Leave Ashburton church and follow northwards into centre	No sign
B	.1	Turn left into North Street, by Lloyds Bank	Widecombe
C	.3	Straight, not left, on to Rew Road	Waterleat
D	.3	Straight, not left, and almost immediately . . .	
		Fork left beyond farm	Waterleat
E	.2	Over small X rds.	Waterleat
F	.6	Straight, not left	Widecombe
	.1	Ashburton Caravan Park on left	
		Up steep hill	
	.5	Through Rushlade hamlet	
G	.3	Turn left at X rds.	Haytor
	.4	On to open moorland	
	.3	Entrance to Ripon Tor Rifle Range on right	
H	.7	Turn right at Cold East Cross Roads	Haytor
		Pil Tor, Hollow Tor and Top Tor over to left	
	.9	Ripon Tor above to right	
I	.5	Turn sharp right	Bovey Tracey
	1.2	Hay Tor on left, Car Park on right	
	.5	Car Park with toilets on right. Guided Walks starting point.	
J	.2	Straight not right by Moorlands Hotel & Craft Centre	Bovey Tracey
K	.1	Fork left just before Hay Tor Service Station	No sign
	.4	Start descending steep hill	
	.5	Yarner Wood National Nature Reserve on right (no entry at this point)	
	.6	Leave open moorland . . . descend steep hill . . .	
	.6	Over stream	
L	.3	Turn right, on to B3344	Becka Falls
M	.1	Arrive Becka Falls Car Park	
		Explore Becka Falls, and TURNABOUT (But go straight ahead if you wish to visit Yarner Wood National Nature Reserve . . 2 miles or go further ahead along B3344 if you wish to visit the Parke Rare Breeds Farm and adjoining National Park Centre — on left after 3 miles)	
L2	.1	Straight, not left, where Manaton entry is signed	Manaton
		Total mileage on this map: 9.8	

CROWN COPYRIGHT RESERVED

On Route

Ashburton

A quiet little town, now remote from the busy main road, Ashburton was an important tin and cloth centre until the coming of the Industrial Revolution. It was also a busy coaching town astride the Exeter–Plymouth road, but the coming of the railways put an effective stop to this activity. Although it has no buildings of outstanding interest, its quiet streets have great charm, with overhung upper storeys and many slate hung walls.

The tall towered church is approached through handsome wrought iron gates, from whence there is a neat yew bordered path to the north door. It was heavily restored by G. E. Street in 1881, and has a stark interior, with scraped and pointed walls, and even the screen is Street's (the medieval screen was apparently used as firewood). However do not overlook the fine monument to John Dunning, 1st Lord Ashburton, in the south transept, nor the beautiful triptych in the north transept, painted by Herbert Read.

Our favourite building in Ashburton is the Methodist Chapel in West Street, with its massive, well painted portico . . . this is 19th century building at its best.

1. West Street, Ashburton

Haytor Rocks

Massive granite outcrop rising over 100 feet above the surrounding moorland heights, providing a splendid viewpoint nearly 1,500 feet above sea level. This is certainly the most dramatic tor lying close to a road, and it is an inevitable place of pilgrimage. However this is set in such a magnificent sweep of country that crowds are absorbed painlessly.

2. Haytor

Becka (or Becky) Falls

Another famous place of pilgrimage, Becka Falls are a true delight to the eye. Situated a short distance from the road, they plunge over and amongst a series of great boulders, a drop of over 70 feet. The volume of water is not usually great enough to create a frighteningly loud or brutal cascade, but the setting amongst the trees completes one of the most beautiful scenes that Dartmoor has to offer. If you must have high drama, postpone your visit here until a few hours after a heavy storm.

There is a pleasant cafe here, which does not intrude upon one's enjoyment of the falls, and the owners have laid out marked walks for the visitor to enjoy the area to the full.

3. The Road towards Yarner Wood

Yarner Wood National Nature Reserve

The entrance is on the Bovey Tracey road two miles beyond Becka Falls (Point M). Turn right after the second cattle grid. Two nature trails start at the car park, where descriptive leaflets are available.

Parke Rare Breeds Farm

This is on left of B3344 about three miles beyond Becka Falls (Point M). Here will be found a comprehensive collection of rare breeds of British farmstock, together with interpretation centres, cafe, gift shop and estate walks.

4. Above Becka Falls

Map 2

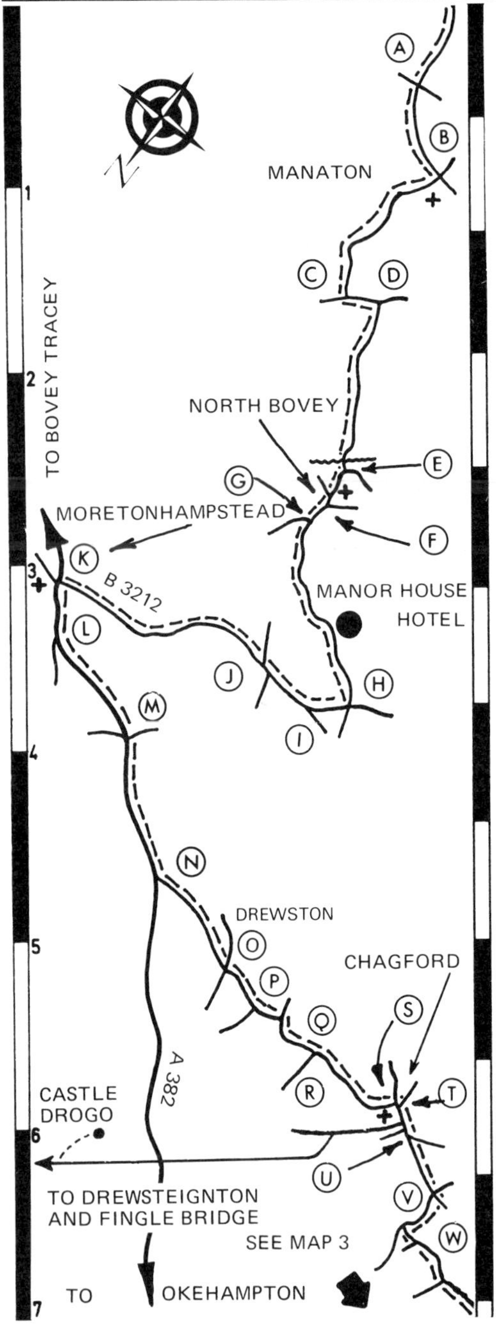

	kms Ref. Miles	Directions	Sign-posted
A	.4	Over X rds. by garage in Manaton	Manaton
B	.5	Turn right at X rds. Church on left	No sign
C	1.1	Turn left at T junction	North Bovey
D	.3	Turn right at T junction	North Bovey
	.8	North Bovey entry signed	
E	.2	Straight, not left, beyond bridge	M'hampstead
	.1	Church on left. Car Park on right	
F	.1	Over X rds. at end of village	Moretonhampstead
G	.1	Straight, not right	No sign
H	1.1	Turn right, on to B3212	Moretonhampstead
I	.3	Straight, not left	M'hampstead
J	.3	Over offset X rds.	M'hampstead
	.7	Moretonhampstead entry signed Keep straight into centre	
K	.7	Fork left and . . .	Chagford
		Turn left, on to A382	Chagford
		Keep out of Moretonhampstead on A382	
L	.3	Bear left, keeping on A382	Okehampton
M	.7	Over small X rds. by bridge	Whiddon Down
N	.8	Fork left off A382 by small house called 'Halfway House'	No sign
	.3	Through Drewston hamlet	
O	.3	Over offset X rds. at Drewstone Cross	Chagford
P	.3	Straight, not right, at bottom of hill (Note model water mill in garden to left)	No sign
Q	.1	Turn right in Gt. Weeke hamlet	Chagford
R	.4	Straight, not right	No sign
	.3	Entering Chagford	
S	.3	Turn right at T junction Then immediately right by church (But Car Park up left, Church on right)	Chagford No sign
T	.1	Straight, not right, in square (But turn right, fork left and cross A382, to visit Castle Drogo, Drewsteignton, or Fingle Bridge . . . see page 9)	Gidleigh
U	.1	Fork right by Moorlands Hotel (BUT FORK LEFT IF YOU WISH TO JOIN MAP 11, POINT C)	Gidleigh
V	.3	Turn right at X rds.	Gidleigh
	.1	Over narrow stone bridge crossing River Teign	
W	.1	Sharp left at T junction, and . . .	Murchington
	.1	Straight, not right at Y junction, and . . .	No sign
		Bear right Total mileage on this map: 10.5	No sign

CROWN COPYRIGHT RESERVED

On Route

Manaton, Bowerman's Nose and Hound Tor

Attractive village on the very edge of the moors. This is overlooked by the dramatic rocky outcrop of Bowerman's Nose, less than a mile to the south-west. (Go straight ahead at Point B, and turn left after about half a mile, before climbing steeply up to the moors. Bowerman's Nose is on the left. Hound Tor lies about a mile further south, to the left of the same road.)

Manaton has a pleasant green surrounded by trees, and overlooked by two long low thatched houses, one of which is the Church House. The nearby church has a tall plastered west tower with obelisk pinnacles, and there are pleasing moorland views from its handsome two storeyed porch. The interior has been extensively restored, but retains its character well. The colourful rood screen stretches right across the church, and there are minute statues around the central doorway.

1. The Ring of Bells, North Bovey

North Bovey

Has by some miracle remained unspoilt despite its popularity with Dartmoor visitors. Perched well above the little River Bovey, It has fine views out over the wooded valley, and to the moorlands beyond. Its thatched cottages look across a green shaded by oaks, with the attractively painted 'Ring of Bells' Inn tucked away in a far corner. The church lies beyond the green in a well tended churchyard.

Its interior, like so many Dartmoor churches, has been much restored, but its atmosphere is enhanced by light from the large plain glass windows. The 15th century screen has attractive statuettes around its central door, as at Manaton (see above), and there is a pleasant series of bench ends.

2. Almshouses at Moretonhampstead

Moretonhampstead

This busy little market town has a pleasing row of 17th century almshouses, complete with a loggia supported on roughly turned granite columns. The church is also of granite and has a fine tower and a large two storeyed porch. However there appears to be little of interest to be seen inside.

Castle Drogo (See Page 9)

3. The Three Crowns, Chagford

Chagford

Small market town below the moors, whose 'ford' across the infant Teign was replaced by a bridge in the 12th or 13th century. Like Ashburton, it prospered as a collecting place for tin from the moorland mines, and later as a cloth centre. It has luckily always been too far from the main valley routes to attract further development, except as a quiet holiday resort. The Three Crowns, which looks out across the street to the churchyard, still has its deep stone porch, where the young poet Sidney Godolphin was killed in a Civil War skirmish in February 1643. The granite church is 15th century, but its interior is dark with Victorian stained glass.

Continued on page 7.

4. Fingle Bridge. (See Route Directions, T.)

Map 3

Directions | Sign-posted

	kms Ref. Miles	Directions	Sign-posted
A	.3	Straight, not right at T junction	Gidleigh
	.1	Straight, not right	Gidleigh
B	1.0	Turn right at T junction	Gidleigh
	.1	Gidleigh church and castle on left	
C	.1	Turn left at T junction	Okehampton
D	.5	Turn sharp right at T junction	Okehampton
E	.5	Turn left at T junction in Moortown hamlet	Okehampton
F	.7	Straight, not right, at T junction	Okehampton
G	.2	Fork right (But go straight ahead along moorland road, if you prefer this to visiting Throwleigh, re-joining route after .9, at Point I)	No sign
H	.8	Straight, not right by Throwleigh church	No sign
I	.8	Straight, not left (Re-joined by moorland road diversion from Point G)	South Zeal
J	.5	Straight, not right	Okehampton
K	.7	Turn left on to A30	Okehampton
L	.4	Straight, at X-rds	Okehampton
	.1	Sticklepath entry signed	
M	.1	Straight, not right	Okehampton
	.3	Finch Foundry Museum on left	
N	.2	Turn sharp left at end of village, off main road	Skaigh
	.6	Turn sharp left	Belstone
O	.7	Turn sharp right (But go straight ahead if you wish to visit Belstone)	No sign
P	.8	Straight over X rds on old A30. (But turn left on old A30 to visit Okehampton and Lydford and on A386 to join at Map 5 Point L.)	Sampford
		Then take bridge over the new A30	
Q	.2	Turn sharp left at X-rds	Chichacott
R	.9	Straight not left by House	No sign
S	.2	Over railway line	
		Total mileage on this map: 10.6	

CROWN COPYRIGHT RESERVED

On Route

Chagford *Continued from Page 5*
In contrast with the dark granite walls there is a pale stone monument in the chancel to Sir John Wyddon (1575), a handsome piece of Renaissance sculpture.

There is a late 19th century flavour about Chagford's square, due no doubt to the discovery of the town by the Victorian 'holiday-maker', and we liked its pleasant little shops and the quaint building with a miniature spire at its centre . . . a real period piece.

Gidleigh

Minute moorland village with a rather dull little 15th century church. Gidleigh Castle close by is in reality the ruins of a fortified manor house. However these are set in a delightful little garden against a backdrop of dark firs, and are in association with the walls of a reputed Saxon manor where the mother of King Harold is believed to have lived (highly conjectural . . . but a nice thought). On the moor above, about a mile to the southwest, is Scorhill, one of Dartmoor's finest prehistoric Stone Circles. (Turn left at Point D, and walk from Berrydown.)

Throwleigh

Delicious little village below the moors, with its church standing well above the road, looking down on a thatched lych gate, and thatched cottages beyond. There is a fine stone surround to the Priest's Door, and inside a large Easter Sepulchre. The 16th century pulpit is made up of parts of an earlier screen, and there is a well carved roof to the chancel. We called here in late summer, and the path to the porch was bordered with nasturtiums, poppies and sunflowers . . . all with the flavour of a cottage garden, and typical of this most pleasing village.
(Note: There are several prehistoric Hut Circles on Throwleigh Moor, beyond Point G on the "Moorland Alternative" . . . See Route Directions.)

Sticklepath

An unexceptional village astride the busy A30, although it is well worth visiting the unusual little Finch Foundry Museum. A team of enthusiasts have restored this fascinating little water-powered foundry, which from 1814 until 1960, produced a wide variety of cutting tools for miners and farmers. Do not miss a visit here.

Belstone

A quiet village on the edge of the moors, with a church almost entirely rebuilt in 1881, an attractive little Gothick 'Telegraph Office', and a hospitable inn called the Tors, which provides meals and accommodation. There are pleasant views southwards to Cawsand Beacon and the northern slopes of Dartmoor. Enquire locally before walking from here in view of the firing range to the south (See Cranmere Pool, Page 9).

1. Gidleigh Castle

2. Throwleigh

3. Open Country near Belstone

4. Early Spring at Belstone

Map 4

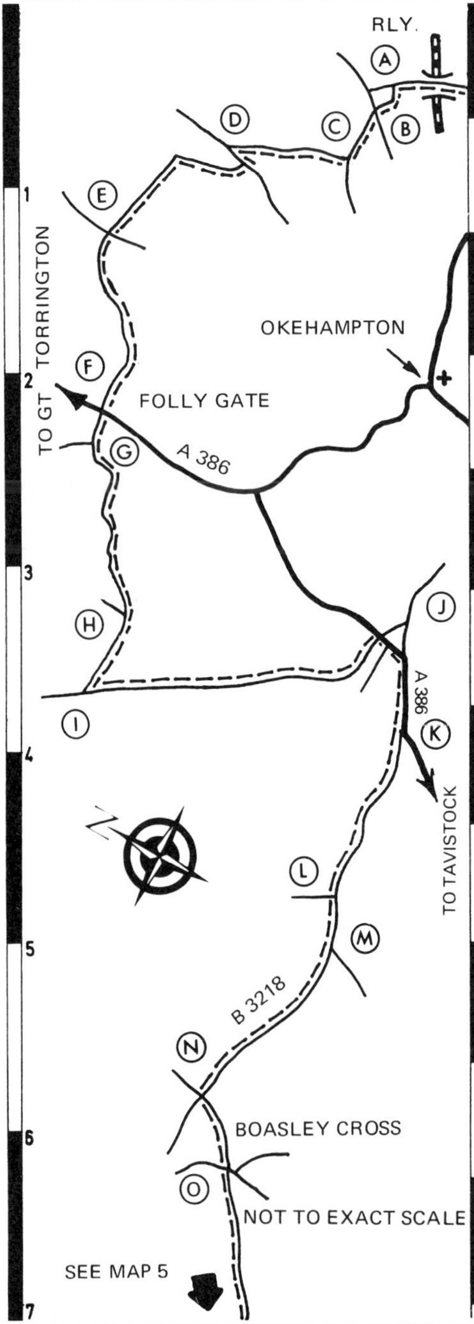

Directions — Signposted

Ref	kms / Miles	Directions	Signposted
A	.3	Turn left at T junction	No sign
B	.2	Over X rds. crossing B3215	No sign
C	.3	Turn right at T junction by farm	No sign
D	.8	Turn left on to B3217	No sign
	.1	Turn right, off B3217, by Priory Cottage	Jacobstowe
		Cross River Okement	
E	.9	Over X rds.	Folly Gate
F	1.2	Over X rds. crossing A386 by the Crossway Inn, at Folly Gate	Inwardleigh
G	.2	Straight, not right	Northlew
	.8	Through ford in wooded area	
H	.3	Straight, not right	No sign
I	.4	Turn sharp left	Okehampton
		Fine views ahead of northern Dartmoor	
J	1.8	Turn right on to A386, and immediately . . .	Tavistock
	.1	Straight, not right, keeping on A386	No sign
	.1	Turn right, keeping on A386	Tavistock
K	.4	Straight, not left, leaving A386, on to B3218	Halwill
L	1.5	Straight, not right	Holsworthy
	.2	Over course of old railway line	
M	.2	Straight, not left	Halwill
N	1.7	Turn left at X rds., leaving B3218	Boasley
O	.5	Straight over 5-way junction keeping right of post box.	Bratton Clovelly
	.7	Over small stream	
		Total mileage on this map: 12.7	

SEE MAP 5

CROWN COPYRIGHT RESERVED

On Route

Bellever Bridge (See Page 22)
The remains of another medieval 'clapper bridge' (see Postbridge, page 23). The road beyond this is quieter than most other moorland roads in summer.

Widecombe-in-the-Moor
An attractive village sheltering in the East Webburn valley, with high moorland on almost every side. It is highly popular with visitors anxious to follow in the well worn footsteps of Uncle Tom Cobbleigh and his friends. Widecombe Fair is still held here on the second Tuesday in September, although it is now mainly a pleasure fair, having little to do with life and work on Dartmoor.

Widecombe church's tall pinnacled tower is one of the finest in Devon and overlooks the little village square, with the 15th century granite Church House on one side, and the Glebe House on the other. The interior of the church is long and low, and contains an interesting series of painted panels, all that remains of the 16th century rood screen. Do not overlook the story of the 1638 'thunderbolt' which can be read on tablets in the church tower.

Widecombe is inevitably popular in high summer, but it is nevertheless well worth visiting, especially if you are able to choose a quieter time of day.

Buckland-in-the-Moor
Charming little thatched village sheltering in a wooded valley with a stream running through some of its cottage gardens. The church has a small west tower complete with turret, and inside there is an interesting painted screen.

Buckland Woods
Here our road plunges steeply down through the lovely Buckland Woods, with the delicious little Webburn River below us on the right. We then cross the Webburn a few yards above the point where it pours into the Dart, here also at its very best. The splendid woods of Holne Chase are on the opposite side of the Dart and access is from our road beyond New Bridge (see below).

New Bridge
Stout 15th century bridge over the Dart, overlooked by high moorlands on one side, and by the woodlands of Holne Chase on the other. Beware of ice cream vans (**and** other motorists) at peak times. We were once foolish enough to try this section on a Sunday afternoon in June, and wished we had stayed beside the Dart in Buckland Woods.

Holne Bridge
Beautiful medieval (1413) bridge over the Dart, with woodlands on every side. Parking in the immediate vicinity very limited.

1. Widecombe Church
2. Cottage by the church, Buckland-in-the-Moor

3. Near Buckland-in-the-Moor

4. At Buckland-in-the-Moor

5. The Dart below New Bridge

Map 13

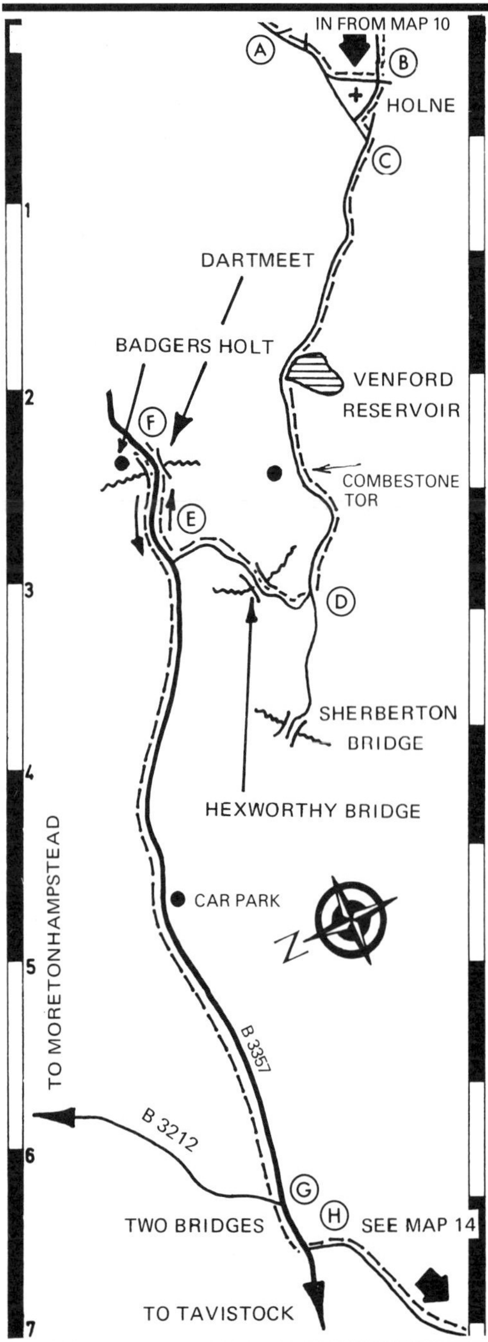

	kms Ref Miles	Directions	Sign-posted
A	.6	Straight, not left, twice	Holne
	.2	Fork left, into Holne village	Holne
B	.2	Turn right at X rds. by the Church House Inn (WE ARE JOINED HERE FROM MAP 10, POINT O)	Hexworthy
	.1	Turn left at T junction	Hexworthy
C	.3	Bear right at T junction	Hexworthy
	.3	Over cattle-grid, and on to open moorland	
	1.1	Over the Venford Reservoir dam	
	1.2	Combestone Tor on right	
	.1	Down 1 in 5 hill	
D	1.0	Fork right (Left fork to Sherberton Bridge not recommended)	Princetown
	.1	Forest Inn on left	
	.4	Over Hexworthy Bridge crossing the Dart	
E	.5	Turn right, on to B3357	Dartmeet
F	.5	Arrive Badger's Holt, Dartmeet, and TURNABOUT	
E2	.5	Straight, not left, keeping on B3357	Princetown
	1.7	Good car park on left	
G	2.1	Straight, not right, keeping on B3357	Tavistock
	.1	Over 'Two Bridges'. Hotel on left	
H	.2	Fork left onto B3212	Plymouth
		Total mileage on this map: 11.4	

CROWN COPYRIGHT RESERVED

On Route

Okehampton

This attractive town below the northern fringes of Dartmoor is well worth the short diversion from our route. It has a long wide street (Fore Street) overlooked by the parish church, from hilly ground some distance westwards. Although the Town Hall, built in 1685 as a private house, is the only really distinguished building in Fore Street, the general effect is pleasing, and there are welcoming shops and hotels. The interesting Museum of Dartmoor is housed in a restored water mill in West Street, and this and the adjoining National Park Information Centre are both part of the Dartmoor Centre, most of which is in an attractive old courtyard with shops and crafts, and a tea room.

Half a mile to the south of the town (well signed from Fore Street) are the interesting remains of Okehampton Castle. These are delightfully situated on a steep little hill commanding the wooded valley of the West Okement River, still fast and fresh from its moorland source. The tall keep is almost certainly Norman in origin, although most of the buildings below it were probably re-built about 1300.

Meldon Reservoir

Drive through Okehampton on A30 and follow sign to the left after about 2 miles, if you wish to visit this attractive reservoir below the moors.

Cranmere Pool

There is a military road up on to Dartmoor leading south from Okehampton to a point not far from Cranmere Pool, but as this lies in the heart of the military training area it is only open at times. For guidance on this point check in Okehampton Post Office where the latest details are available.

Cranmere Pool is the source of the West Okement River and is also situated close to the sources of the rivers, Taw, Dart, Teign and Tavy, and together with the bogs in its vicinity Cranmere is in effect the 'Great Source' of Devon's principal rivers.

Before the coming of the military road, Cranmere was the wildest and most remote place on Dartmoor, and for over a hundred years it has been the objective of most serious moorland walkers. Even now it is advisable to keep clear of this area after wet weather, as the Pool is almost surrounded by boggy fen-like country and walking can be exhausting and unpleasant. Always carry a compass and a 1:50,000 or 1:25,000 Ordnance Survey Map if you aim to move any distance away from moorland roads.

Castle Drogo (N.T.) (See Page 4)

Splendid granite 'castle' built by the celebrated architect Sir Edwin Lutyens between 1910 and 1930, on a dramatic crag standing 900 feet above the thickly wooded gorge of the Teign. Terraced gardens, woodland walks, restaurant. Drive on beyond the entrance to Castle Drogo for Drewsteignton and the delightful Fingle Bridge. (For details see *South Devon by Car*.)

1. In Okehampton

2. Okehampton Castle

3. Our road towards Bratton Clovelly

4. Castle Drogo (See Page 4)   National Trust Photograph

Map 5

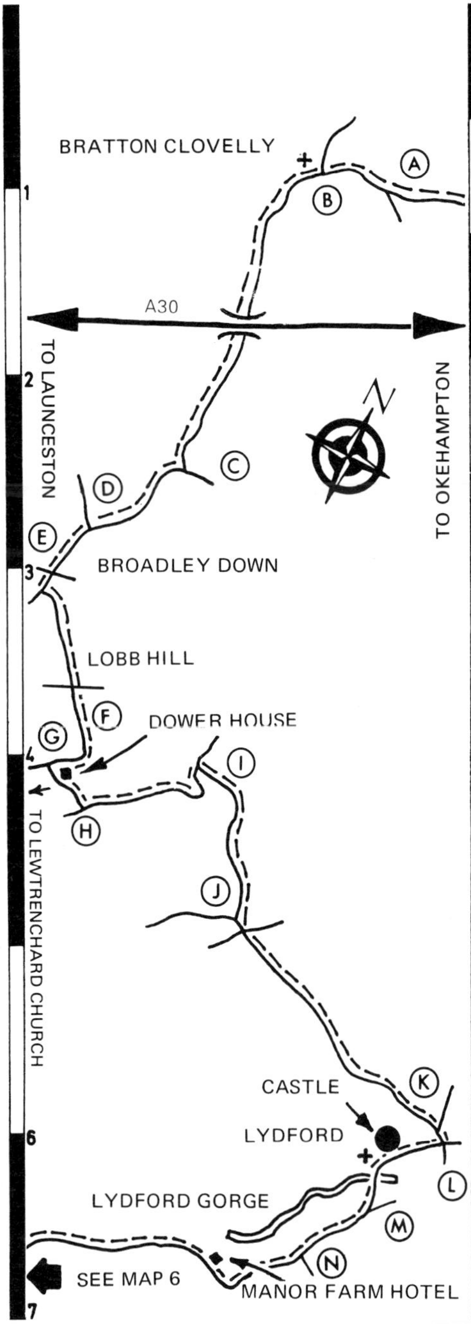

Ref.	kms / Miles	Directions	Signposted
A	1.0	Straight, not left	No sign
	.6	Bratton Clovelly entry signed	
B	.3	Straight, not right, by church and Post Office	Lewdown
	1.4	Under bridge beneath A30	
C	.6	Turn right at T junction	Lewdown
D	.6	Straight, not right	Lewdown
E	.4	Over small X rds. in Broadley Down hamlet	Tavistock
	.1	Turn left at T junction (Watch for this with care)	Broadley Chapel
F	.6	Over X rds at Lobb Hill Cross (VERY DANGEROUS. GREAT CARE REQUIRED)	No sign
G	.6	Turn sharp left into road lined with trees (Watch for this with care) (But go straight ahead if you wish to visit Lewtrenchard church . . . about 1 mile)	No sign
	.1	Lew Mill Dower House on left	
H	.3	Turn left at T junction	No sign
	.7	Farm on right, as we bear to left	
I	.2	Sharp turn right up hill	Lydford
J	.9	Turn left at T junction	No sign
	.1	Straight over X rds.	Lydford
		Good view of Dartmoor ahead	
K	1.6	Straight, not left, at entry to Lydford	Lydford
L	.1	Turn right by cross	Brentor
	.3	Lydford Castle and Church on right	
		Car Park on left	
	.2	Main entrance to Lydford Gorge on right. Large Car Park and Shop.	
M	.2	Sharp turn right after passing under first railway bridge	Brentor
N	.3	Straight, not left	No sign
	.4	Over second railway bridge	
	.2	Over third railway bridge	
		Manor Farm Hotel on right	
	.1	Second entrance to Lydford Gorge with Car Park and NT kiosk.	
		Total mileage on this map: 12.0	

CROWN COPYRIGHT RESERVED

On Route

Bratton Clovelly

An exceedingly rural and unspoilt village built on a small hill, with houses and roadways all on different levels, and with fine views over rolling countryside towards the western flanks of Dartmoor. The 14th century church has a splendid medieval south door (we thought it locked until we persevered, so do not be deterred). Inside there is beautiful tall arcading, and a magnificent tower arch. The whole interior has a feeling of spacious height, and is most pleasing. Its contents include wall paintings in the north aisle, and a Norman font with grotesque figures at its corners. On leaving the church do not miss the beautifully lettered tombstone outside the south door to Mary Williams (1788), headed by the words 'Reader, improve thy precious time'.

1. *Bratton Clovelly Church*

Lewtrenchard

The Dower House is an interesting stone building by the little River Lew, and has the date 1664 carved upon one of its lintels. The village of Lewtrenchard lies about a mile to the west of our route (go straight ahead at Point G), beyond pleasant woods. The church is attractively sited below woodlands and is worth visiting for its interesting series of bench ends. The Rev. Baring-Gould, novelist, hymnologist and antiquarian, was rector here for 30 years.

2. *Lydford Keep*

Lydford

Now a small village, but it has a long and important history, dating back to the establishment of a fortified Borough and a mint in Anglo-Saxon times. Situated on a promontory it was originally defended by an earthen bank to the north-east. The castle, a tall square keep overlooking a deep gorge, was built in 1195, and was used primarily to imprison offenders against the laws of the Forest, and the Stannaries (an organisation regulating the mining activities of the region, and for many years almost outside the rule of normal law). Grim stories are told of imprisonment, starvation and death, sometimes without trial, in Lydford Keep, and an oft quoted 17th century jingle read thus:

> I oft have heard of Lydford Law,
> How in the morn they hang and draw . . .
> And sit in judgement after.

The village of Lydford itself is not exceptional, although the Castle Inn is prettily decked out, and stands close to the castle on its well mown motte. Beyond the castle lies the church, a mixture of Early English and Perpendicular styles, with a dark heavily restored interior. Near the south door stands the well known tombstone of the watchmaker (1802) inscribed with a heavily humorous epitaph rounded off with these words:

> "Wound up in the hopes of being taken in hand
> by his maker and of being thoroughly cleaned,
> repaired and set a 'going in a world to come'."

3. *The Castle Inn, Lydford*

However the best of Lydford lies a few yards beyond the village, for it is here that the first entrance to Lydford Gorge is situated. The Gorge, *Continued on page 13.*

4. *Lydford Gorge*

Map 6

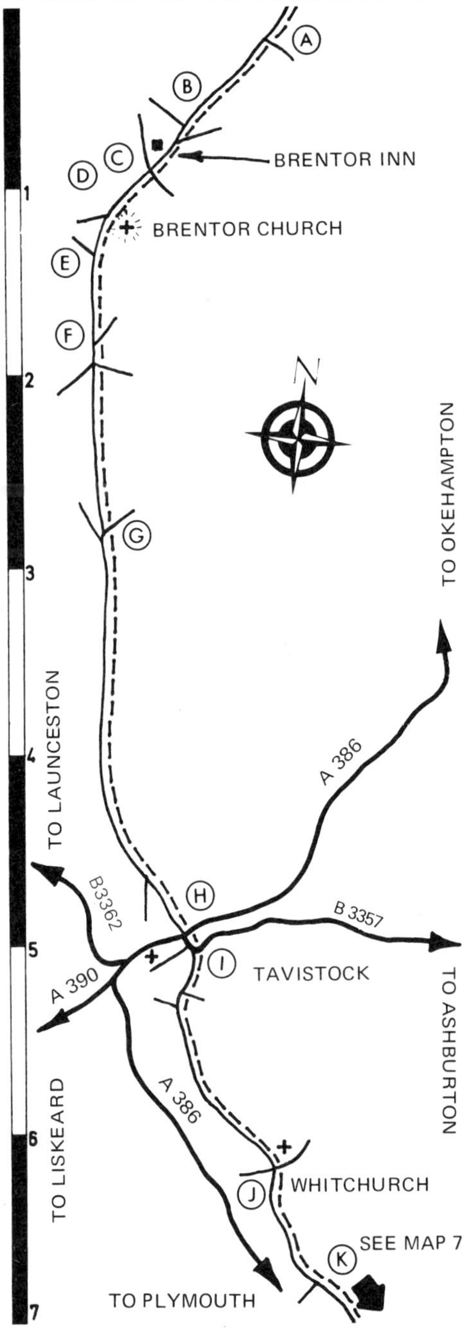

Ref.	Miles	Directions	Sign-posted
	1.4	Entry to Brentor signed, but no sign of village	
A	.1	Straight, not left	Tavistock
B	.6	Straight, not right	Tavistock
	.1	Straight, not left	Tavistock
C	.2	Over X rds. by the Brentor Inn	Milton Abbot
D	.3	Straight not right (But turn right for Brentor Church Car Park)	Tavistock
	.1	Brentor Church on left	
E	.3	Straight, not right	Tavistock
F	.5	Straight, not left	No sign
	.1	Over X rds.	Tavistock
G	.9	Straight, not left	No sign
	.1	Straight, not right	Tavistock
	1.9	Enter Tavistock	
		Follow into Tavistock centre	
		Under large viaduct, and ...	
H	.5	Over main X rds. in Tavistock centre	No sign
		Church on right	
		Straight, not right, near the Bedford Hotel	Princetown
	.1	Straight, not left beyond Car Park	
		Cross River Tavy and ...	
I	.1	Bear right, up hill by Abbey Garage, on to Whitchurch Road	Whitchurch
		Keep straight out of Tavistock on this road	
J	1.3	Over X rds. by 'Pooh Corner' House, in Whitchurch (But turn left if you wish to visit church)	Plymouth
K	.6	Straight, not right in Grenofen hamlet	No sign
		Total mileage on this map: 8.5	

CROWN COPYRIGHT RESERVED

On Route

Lydford Gorge *Continued from page 11* which is complete with fast flowing stream, is about 1½ miles in length and wonderfully wooded. Near the far end is the 100 foot high White Lady Waterfall, and it is possible to re-join the road again at Manor Farm. (See Route Details.) This is one of Devon's outstandingly beautiful walks and should not on any account be missed.

Brentor

An isolated volcanic outcrop (not a granite tor) which is dramatically topped by a little 13th century church, standing at 1130 feet above sea level. Brentor is a striking landmark, and those who climb up to its little church will be rewarded by splendid views, on the one side, of the western flanks of Dartmoor, and on the other, out over the broad Tamar valley to the distant Moors of Bodmin.

1. Brentor Church

Tavistock

Tavistock is the creation of its two owners . . . the Abbots of Tavistock Abbey and later the Earls and Dukes of Bedford. A great Benedictine abbey was founded here in 974 and its abbots created a town, which grew prosperous in the middle ages with the tin mining activity of South West Dartmoor, then Europe's most extensive source of this metal. At the dissolution of the monasteries in 1539 the abbey and its estates passed to the Earl of Bedford and the development of the town relied upon his heirs for nearly 400 years. By the 17th century the cloth trade had taken the place of tin, but unlike the other Dartmoor towns of Ashburton and Chagford, Tavistock's decline was more than offset by the development of copper mining. This industry reached its peak in the 1860s, but had almost died out by the turn of the century.

2. Tavistock Church

The appearance of present day Tavistock is due largely to the re-moulding activities of the 7th Duke of Bedford, who re-built much of the town in the days of the copper boom. The buildings are rather grey and severe, but the overall plan is pleasing, and there is lively, colourful activity in the town's shopping streets. Remains of the great abbey are only fragmentary and to piece them together is an architectural exercise beyond our scope. Let us concentrate instead on the pleasant riverside walk beside the Tavy, the two handsome 18th century bridges, and the large parish church. The latter has a spacious, finely proportioned interior, mainly 15th century in origin. The outer south aisle known as the Clothworkers Aisle, was built in 1445 and has a beautiful wagon roof.

For details of the fascinating Morwellham Quay Centre, which lies about four miles to the south-west of Tavistock, see our companion guide, *Plymouth Country by Car*.

3. The Tavy at Tavistock

Whitchurch

Village on the outskirts of Tavistock with a largely Perpendicular church, heavily restored by the Victorians. Full marks to the owner of 'Little Dumplings' . . . a house name with a difference.

4. Sir Francis Drake, Tavistock

5. Francis, Duke of Bedford, Tavistock

Map 7

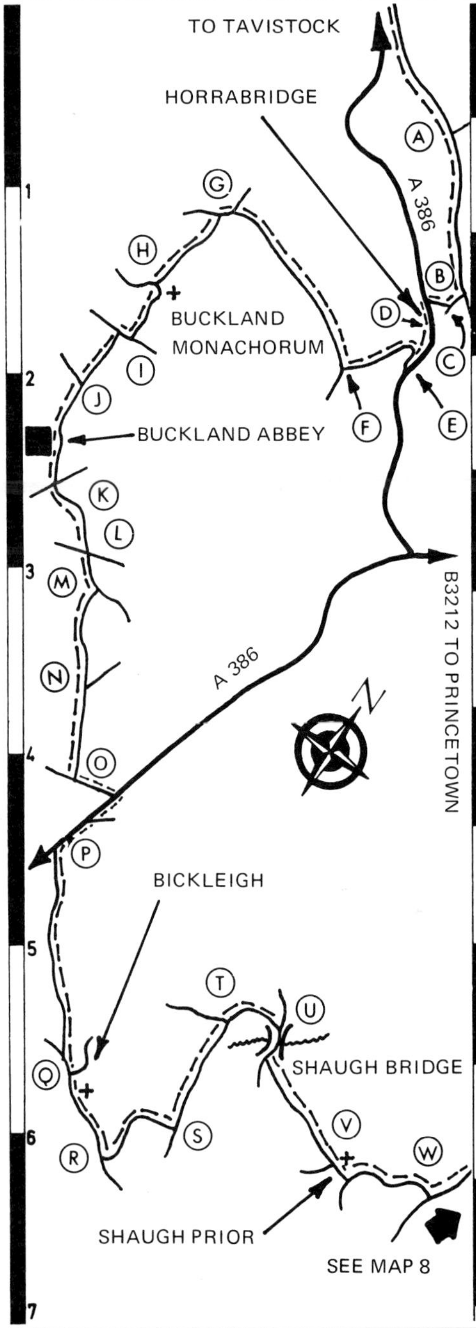

	kms Ref. Miles	Directions	Sign-posted
A	.2	Straight not right	No sign
	1.1	Entry to Horrabridge signed	
B	.5	Turn right at T junction, and cross Medieval Bridge	No sign
C	.3	Keep straight passing several turnings on housing estate	No sign
D	.1	Turn left with care on to A386	No sign
E	.5	Turn sharp right off A386	Crapstone
F	.5	Turn right at T junction	Coppice Town
G	1.2	Turn left at offset X rds.	Buckland
	.4	Enter Buckland Monachorum	
H	.1	Turn left at T junction	No sign
	.1	Bear round right, church on left	No sign
I	.3	Turn right at T junction at end of village	No sign
	.1	Turn left at T junction	Milton Combe
J	.3	Straight, not right, at T junction	Buckland Abbey
K	.6	Over X rds. (But turn sharp right to visit Buckland Abbey)	Roborough
L	.4	Over X rds.	Roborough
M	.2	Straight, not left after crossing bridge, and . . . Bear round to the right	No sign
N	.3	Straight, not left, by entry to open moorland	Plymouth
O	.5	Turn left at X rds.	Plymouth
	.2	Turn right with care on to A386	Plymouth
	.2	Straight, not left at Y junction, keeping on A386	Plymouth
	.2	Straight, not right, keeping on A386	No sign
P	.1	Turn left at T junction, off A386, and . . . Over cattle-grid	No sign
Q	1.1	Turn left, on to wider road, and almost immediately . . . Straight, not left	No sign
	.1	Bickleigh entry signed	
	.1	Straight, not left by church	
R	.3	Turn left at T junction beyond barrack area	Shaugh Prior
S	.6	Bear left at T junction at bottom of hill	Shaugh Prior
T	.8	Bear right at T junction in woods	No sign
U	.4	Turn right at T junction in woods Past Car Park, and over Shaugh Bridge	Shaugh Prior
	.1	Keep straight, not right	Shaugh Prior
	.4	Shaugh Prior entry signed	
V	.3	Straight not right	No sign
	.1	Turn left at T junction	Cadover Bridge
W	.6	Bear left at T junction	Yelverton
	.3	Flooded clay pit over to right	
		Total mileage on this map: 13.2	

CROWN COPYRIGHT RESERVED

On Route

Horrabridge
Nondescript sprawl with a late Victorian church. However it has an interesting medieval bridge over the little River Walkham.

Buckland Monachorum
Attractive village in rolling countryside between Roborough Down and the wooded Tavy estuary. We particularly liked the prettily painted 'Drake Manor' Inn and the mellow little 'Lady Modford's School' (1702), with its stone mullioned windows looking out over the churchyard. The late Perpendicular church has been over restored, but the Drake Aisle alone justifies a visit here. It is believed that it was built soon after Sir Francis Drake's purchase of Buckland Abbey and it contains a fine monument to one of his descendants, Sir Francis Henry Drake (1794) and to Lord Heathfield (1795), who married into the Drake family. John Bacon was the sculptor of both.

1. Medieval Bridge, Horrabridge

Buckland Abbey
A Cistercian abbey established in 1278, overlooking the lovely wooded shores of the Tavy estuary, and colonised from Quarr Abbey in the Isle of Wight. Following the Dissolution it was sold to Sir Richard Grenville, whose grandson Sir Richard (of the Revenge) sold it to Sir Francis Drake in 1581. Twelve generations of Drakes made Buckland their home, and it only passed out of their hands in 1946. It now belongs to the National Trust.

2. Beyond Horrabridge

The abbey church was successfully converted into a fine Elizabethan mansion and now houses a fascinating museum, including Drake relics, Devon Folk material, and an excellent collection of ship models. Close to the house there is a 14th century tithe barn, whose splendidly spacious interior contains carriages, carts, an old fire engine and a massive 18th century cider press. Teas and light meals are available in the 'Kitchen'.

Bickleigh
Situated to the immediate west of the beautifully wooded Plym valley, Bickleigh struggles to survive against the onslaught of service camp and pylon line. Apart from the tall Perpendicular tower, the rest of the church was re-built in 1829, at the expense of Sir Manasseh Lopes, a West Indian sugar planter, whose monument is inside.

3. Buckland Abbey

Shaugh Bridge
Beautiful woodlands surround this meeting place of the Meavy and the Plym, and oak trees overhang the boulder strewn stream beds. Walk up to the Dewerstone, a hundred foot high, sheer cliff, above which is an Iron Age hill fort.

Shaugh Prior
Perched on the very fringe of the moor, Shaugh looks down south-westwards to Plymouth, and we envied the view from the snug little terrace of cottages close to the church. The latter is a rather severe granite building, but contains a splendid 16th century font cover, having a two storeyed octagon with pointed top.

4. Shaugh Bridge

Map 8

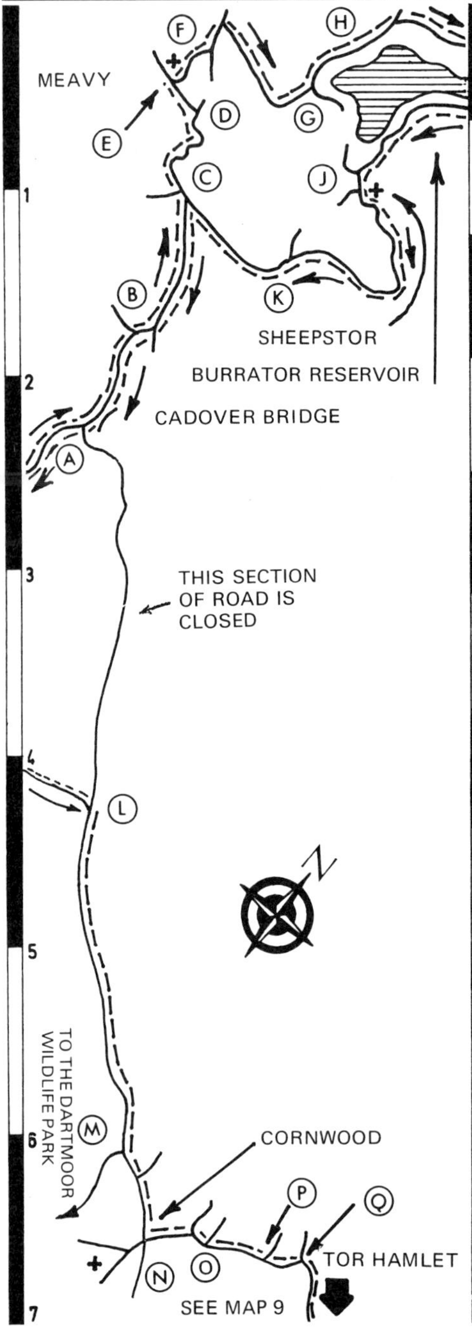

Ref	kms/Miles	Directions	Sign-posted
A	.5	Straight, not right, and over Cadover Bridge	Yelverton
B	.6	Turn right onto minor road	Meavy
	.1	Turn left at T junction	No sign
C	.8	Over offset X rds.	Meavy
	.5	Over attractive bridge, near ford and stepping stones	
D	.1	Turn left at T junction at entry to Meavy	Yelverton
E	.3	Turn sharp right at T junction by village green	No sign
F	.3	Left at T junction	No sign
	.1	Turn sharp right onto open moorland	Burrator
G	.8	Straight, not right, by Burrator Reservoir Dam (We shall now almost encircle the Reservoir)	No sign
H	.4	Fork right	No sign
	.9	Sharpitor above on left	
I	.2	Straight, not left	No sign
J	1.9	Turn left at T junction	No sign
	.1	Straight, not right, by Sheepstor Church	No sign
	.2	Bear right	No sign
	.4	Bear right	Ivybridge
K	.8	Straight, not right, at Y junction	No sign
C2	.7	Turn sharp left, at offset X rds., thus rejoining our route at Point C	Cadover
	.8	Turn right at T junction	No sign
B2	1	Fork left	Cadover Bridge
	.5	Over Cadover Bridge, and...	
A2		Keep right beyond bridge, retracing our route, as road to left is blocked	Shaugh Prior
		NOW OFF MAP	
	.8	Straight, not right	No sign
	.6	Turn left at X-rds.	Wotter
	.5	Straight not left	No sign
	.5	Straight not left	No sign
	.7	Straight at staggered X rds.	Cornwood
		NOW BACK ON MAP	
L	2.1	Straight not right at T-junction, re-joining our original route (But turn right, then turn right again, through Lutton and well beyond, if you wish to visit the Dartmoor Wildlife Park, which is on right . . . 1.8)	Cornwood
	.1	Straight, not left	No sign
	.1	Cornwood entry sign	
N	.2	Turn left at X rds. in Cornwood (But turn right, and fork left to visit church)	Harford
O	.3	Bear right at T junction	No sign
	.1	Straight, not left	No sign
P	.3	Straight, not left beyond small bridge	Harford
Q	.3	Turn right in Tor hamlet Total mileage on this map: 17.1	

CROWN COPYRIGHT RESERVED

On Route

Cadover Bridge
An undistinguished bridge over the little river Plym. The nearby china clay mines detract from the wild moorland scene, but there is fine walking up the Plym valley.

Brisworthy
(Half a mile to the right of T junction beyond Point B.)
It was here that there was the first recorded tin mining settlement (12th century). No trace of this activity now remains.

Marchants Cross
An interesting medieval cross on the right of our road a few yards before the ford. (See route directions.)

Meavy
Has an attractive village green dominated by a massive oak. This looks pretty sick, and despite extensive propping, leans heavily over towards the lych gate. The thin towered granite church has Norman origins, but it is not very exciting. The nearby Royal Oak Inn has the rugged appeal of the true Free House, and has so far escaped the attentions of prettifying brewery decorators.

Burrator Reservoir (See Page 31)

Sheepstor
Situated in moorland below Sheeps Tor, and only a short distance beyond Burrator Reservoir, its setting is probably the finest of all the Dartmoor villages. The church is approached by a solid little lych gate beside the 16th century Church House, and has a pleasantly pinnacled tower. Inside there is a dark little Victorian chancel and a delightful monument in marble to Elizabeth Elford (1641).

Be sure to read the interesting story of the Brookes, the Rajahs of Sarawak, on a tablet in the church. Rajah Brooke and his nephew, the second Rajah, are both buried in the churchyard. How remote from the humid lushness of the East Indies it all seems.

Route Amendment
We are sorry about alteration of the return route between A2 and L, which is due to a blocking of the original route. We are not yet sure if this will ever be re-opened, but have left our map largely unchanged with this thought in mind.

The Dartmoor Wildlife Park
This is situated in the grounds of Goodamoor House, and there are fine views towards the coast. The 25 acre park contains a wide variety of British and European animals and birds; and many free flying waterfowl, together with pheasants and rabbits, mingle with the visitors.

Cornwood
The village itself is unexceptional, although the parish of Cornwood is one of the largest on Dartmoor, stretching far up into the moors, and covering an area over 10,000 acres. There is good walking up on these moors and prehistoric remains in plenty. The large Perpendicular church contains three

Continued on page 19.

1. Ford near Marchant's Cross

2. The Royal Oak, Meavy

3. Burrator Reservoir Dam

4. At the Dartmoor Wildlife Park

Map 9

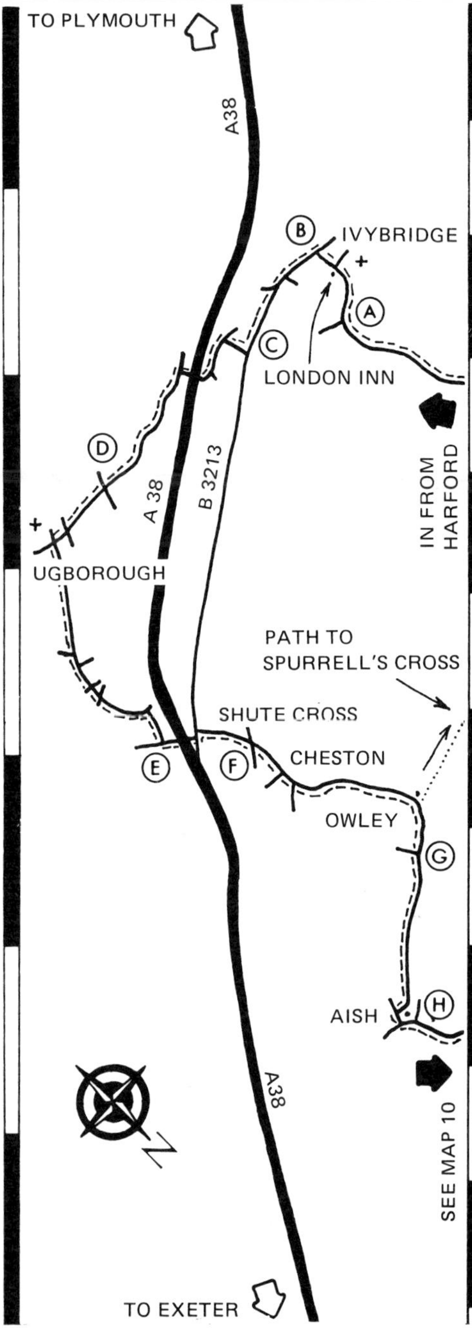

Ref.	kms / Miles	Directions	Sign-posted
		NOT ON MAP	
	1.7	Bear right beyond Harford church	Ivybridge
A	1.9	Over railway bridge, and . . .	No sign
		Straight at X-rds	No sign
	.5	Straight, not right by London Hotel and old bridge	No sign
B	.1	Turn left, on to B3213 and immediately straight not right at roundabout	Exeter Exeter
		Keep on the B3213 passing estate roads on right and left	
C	1.0	Turn right at X rds. by phone box, off B3213 (WATCH FOR THIS WITH CARE)	No sign
	.1	Turn left at small T junction	No sign
	.2	Straight, not left, and . . .	No sign
		Over bridge, crossing A38	
	.1	Bear left at T junction	No sign
	.4	Bear left and over small bridge	No sign
D	.7	Over X rds.	Ugborough
	.4	Over X rds. at entry to Ugborough	No sign
	.1	Turn left at entry to village square, and . . .	No sign
		Pass Anchor Inn on left	
	.7	Straight, not right	Wrangaton
	.1	Straight, not left	No sign
	.1	Over X rds., and . . .	Wrangaton
		Fork left	No sign
	.3	Fork right near large pylon	No sign
E	.2	Turn left at T junction on to B3196	No sign
	.2	Over bridge, crossing A38	
	.1	Turn left at T junction, on to B3213, and immediately . . .	Bittaford
		Turn right off B3213	No sign
F	.3	Over Shute Cross roads	Cheston
	.3	Straight, not right, in Cheston hamlet, and . . .	Owley
		Fork left	Owley
	.8	Through Owley hamlet	
G	.3	Straight, not right, and immediately straight not left	No sign
	1.0	Turn left at T junction	No sign
	.1	Turn left at T junction beyond riding stables	Didworthy
H	.1	Bear right at end of Aish hamlet	No sign
		Total mileage on this map: 11.8	

CROWN COPYRIGHT RESERVED

On Route

Cornwood *Continued from page 17*
interesting 17th century monuments. One wonders why the inscription on that of Robert and Dorothy Bellmaine was inscribed.

> Here's rest and peace
> Within the grave,
> Which we in life
> Could never have.

Harford

The gateway to the beautiful moorland section of the Erme valley, Harford is the natural starting point for walks northwards up this valley, or westwards across the 1,200 foot high shoulder of moor land to Spurrell's Cross, and Owley hamlet beyond (see below). The moors on either side of the Erme are particularly rich in Bronze Age remains, with Stone Rows, Enclosures, and Hut Circles.

Harford church stands in a simple churchyard overlooking the gloriously wooded Erme valley. There is a long path to the south door, overhung with beech trees. Dating from the 15th and 16th centuries, it is a church full of atmosphere inside, with much plain glass. There is an altar tomb with brasses, to Thomas Williams, who became Speaker of the House of Commons in 1536, and a monument to John and Agnes, the parents of John Prideaux, Bishop of Worcester (1538 – 1650).

Elizabeth Chudleigh (1720 – 1788), self-styled Duchess of Kingston, was born here at nearby Hall Farm. Described in the Dictionary of National Biography as 'beautiful, but weak minded and illiterate', she followed a career of marital and extra-marital adventures that appears to have shocked even the broad minded aristocracy of 18th century Europe.

Do not miss this delightfully situated village, with its church and farms deep in the wooded valley . . all in great contrast to the high moorlands away beyond it.

Ugborough

A large village whose wide open square with a conduit at its centre, has a feel of Brittany about it . . . Perhaps it is the multiplicity of electric cables that prompts us to make comparison. The church and churchyard stand above the square and are surrounded by an earthwork, which is probably prehistoric. The church has an impressive west tower, and its north door is approached by a long flight of steps up from the square.

Inside there is a pleasing stone flagged floor (what a relief after the dismal succession of red, glossy Victorian tiles in the churches we have been looking at earlier), high pointed arcading, an unusual 17th century stone pulpit, a low screen with medieval figures, and a roof in the north aisle with a splendid series of carved bosses, one of which depicts St. Brannoc's sow with her litter.

Owley

Minute hamlet below the moors, with a path heading westwards over to Spurrell's Cross and Harford (see above).

1. Harford Bridge

2. Harford Churchyard

3. The Old Bridge, Ivybridge

4. Ugborough Tower

5. Farm beyond Cheston

Map 10

Ref.	kms / Miles	Directions	Sign-posted
A	.5	Fork right	No sign
B	.5	Straight, not left, and . . . Straight not right	Avon Dam South Brent
	.6	Car Park on left. Walk to Avon Dam from here	
	.1	Over Shipley Bridge	
C	1.4	Straight, not right	South Brent
	.2	Bear left at T junction	Gidley
	.9	Over Gidley Bridge	
D	.2	Turn left at T junction and immediately . . .	No sign
		Turn sharp right	No sign
	.3	Straight not left at Y junction	No sign
E	1.0	Bear left by Deancombe Farm, and immediately . . .	No sign
		Turn left at T junction	Buckfastleigh
F	.5	Straight, not right	No sign
G	.3	Over small X rds.	Buckfastleigh
	.4	Straight, not right, joining wider road	'Duckspond Road'
	.2	Straight, not left, at Y junction, and immediately . . .	Buckfastleigh
		Turn right at T junction	Town Centre
	.3	Turn left at T junction near St. Luke's Church	No sign
	.1	Bear right by Globe Inn	'Fore Street'
	.1	Left into one-way system	No sign
	.1	Bear left into Dart Bridge Rd	Buckfast Abbey
	.1	Buckfast Station (DVR) on right	
H	.3	Turn left just **before** Dart Bridge	Buckfast Abbey
	.5	Turn left at mini roundabout before abbey gate	No sign
		Car Park for Abbey on right	
	.1	Right at T junction	Buckfast
		Drive round edge of estate	
I	.2	Turn left, and . . .	No sign
		Straight, not left	No sign
J	.5	Turn right, and almost immediately left	No sign
K	.3	Turn right at X rds.	Holne
L	1.3	Straight not left by old cross, and . . .	No sign
		Straight over X rds.	Holne
M	.3	Straight not left . . . over stream . . .and turn right	Holne
N	.4	Straight, not right	Holne
	.3	Turn left at T junction	Holne
	.3	Entry to Holne signed	
O	.1	Turn right at X rds. by the Church House Inn (BUT GO OVER X-RDS FOLLOWING SIGN TO PRINCETOWN IF YOU WISH TO JOIN MAP 13, AT POINT B)	Ashburton
	.1	Bear right at T junction	Ashburton
P	.2	Straight, not right	Ashburton
	.2	Straight, not right	Ashburton
Q	.3	Bear left at T junction	Ashburton
R	.3	Fork right	Ashburton
S	.2	Bear right	Ashburton
	.7	Bear left, and over Holne Bridge,	Ashburton
	.6	Bear right	Ashburton
	.7	River Dart Country Park entrance on right	
T	.4	Fork left just before garage on right	Ashburton
U	.5	Arrive Ashburton Church (LINK WITH MAP 1, POINT A) Total mileage on this map: 16.7	

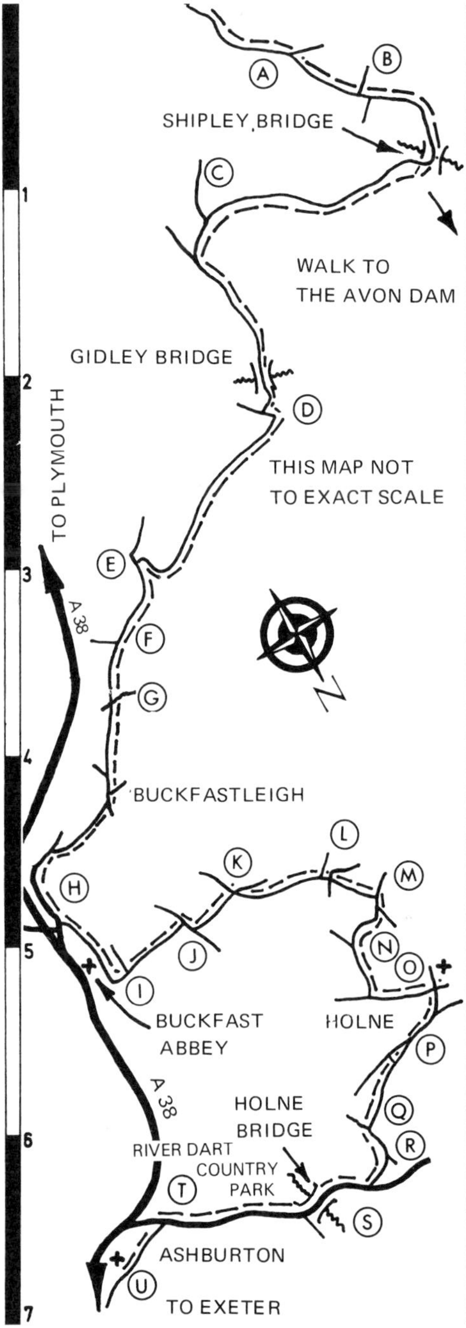

CROWN COPYRIGHT RESERVED

On Route

The Avon Dam
There is a car park at Shipley Bridge (½ mile beyond Point B) and from here it is about a two mile walk up the road to the reservoir formed by the Avon Dam. Although this may be regarded as yet another encroachment upon the solitude of the moor it provides an attractive and interesting walk. There are wildfowl to be spotted here in winter.

Buckfastleigh
Small market town long overshadowed by Ashburton, and like Ashburton, bypassed by the busy A38. It must also have suffered commercially when Buckfast Abbey was dissolved in 1539.

Dart Valley Railway
Closed by British Railways in 1962, it was reopened by the Dart Valley Light Railway Company between Buckfastleigh and Totnes in 1969. The line follows the north bank of the Dart for its entire course.

Buckfast Abbey
A Cistercian Abbey stood here between the years 1148 and 1539 (when all monastic houses were 'dissolved' by Henry VIII), but it was soon stripped and allowed to fall into ruins. A woollen mill and a house were built here in the early 19th century, but the site was purchased by Benedictines from France in 1882. Between 1906 and 1938 a small group of monks, never more than six at a time, undertook, with the assistance of an architect, the building of the abbey that we see today.

Although a little cold in appearance Buckfast Abbey is an undeniably impressive building, and the achievement of these truly inspired men is an example that should not be overlooked in this age of instant everything. Do not overlook the beautiful Blessed Sacrament Chapel, with its brilliant coloured glass (also the work of the monks).

The community at Buckfast numbers fifty brothers and they have created a fine tourist attraction. Three gift shops offer a variety of the Abbey's produce, and another shop sells carpets made of wool from the mill.

Hembury Castle and Hembury Woods
(Turn right at Point J and keep right, for this diversion off our route.)

After a short distance we enter the lovely Hembury Woods*, the property of the National Trust. Hembury Castle is an Iron Age hill fort on a summit about 500 feet above sea level, from whence there are splendid views of the Dart valley. There is also a delightful pathway alongside the Dart, at the foot of the woods. To re-join the route, keep left all the time, and you will arrive at Holne (Point O).

*There is a nature trail through Hembury Woods.

River Dart Country Park
Here in Holne Park, beside the lovely river Dart, there is swimming, pony and donkey rides, flyfishing, nature trails and woodland walks. During the holiday season there is a shop and cafeteria.

Holne (See Page 27)

Holne Bridge (See Page 25)

1. Shipley Bridge

2. Buckfast Abbey

3. Holne Bridge

Map 11

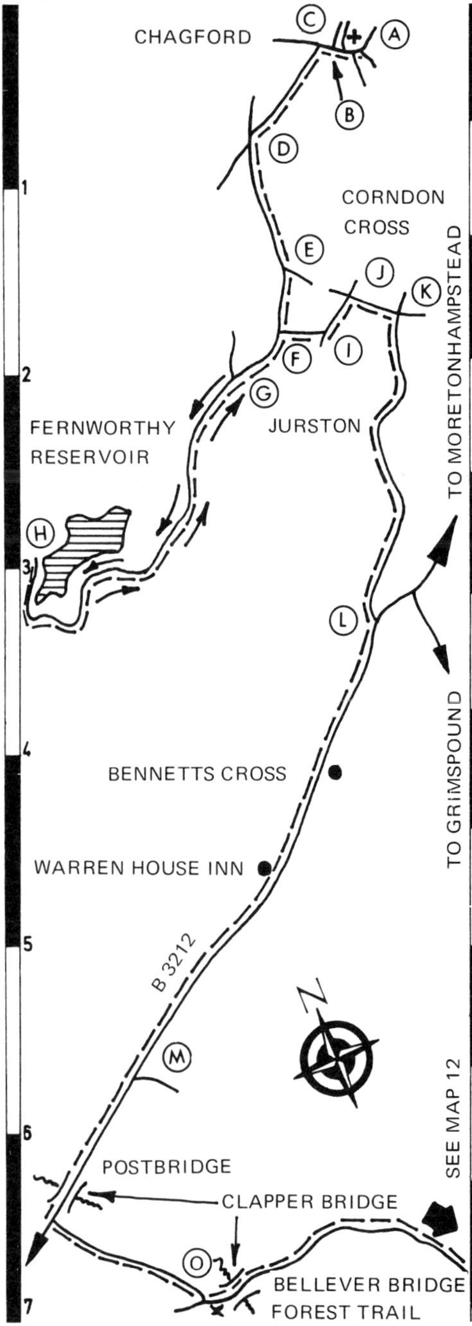

Directions / Signposted

Ref.	kms/Miles	Directions	Signposted
A		Leave Chagford church and proceed down street, with Three Crowns Inn on left	No sign
B	.1	Straight, not right in square	Gidleigh
C	.1	Fork left by Moorlands Hotel (THIS POINT IS COMMON WITH MAP 2, POINT U)	Fernworthy
D	.7	Bear left at T junction, and almost immediately . . .	No sign
		Straight, not right	Fernworthy
E	.7	Fork right to visit Fernworthy Reservoir	Fernworthy
F	.3	Straight, not left	Fernworthy
G	.4	Straight, not right. (Do not be deterred by 'NO THROUGH ROAD' sign)	Fernworthy
	1.3	Fernworthy Reservoir on right. Woods on left with Car Parks, and Forest Walks	
	.6	Prehistoric Hut Circle on left	
H	.7	Arrive at end of road and TURNABOUT	
G2	2.6	Straight, not left	Chagford
F2	.4	Turn right at T junction	Corndon
I	.2	Turn left at T junction by P.O. Box	No sign
J	.3	Turn right at Corndon Cross	Princetown
K	.3	Turn right at X rds.	Princetown
	.5	Through Jurston hamlet, and climb up on to the moors	
L	1.3	Bear right on to B3212 (But turn sharp left, and after .2, sharp right to visit Grimspound — see opposite)	Princetown
	1.0	Bennett's Cross on left	
	.5	Warren House Inn on right	
M	1.4	Straight, not left, near Postbridge entry sign	No sign
	.5	Postbridge church on left	
	.3	East Dart Hotel on left	
		Over Bridge (Clapper Bridge to the left)	
		Car Park beyond on right	
N	.2	Turn left, off B3212, and over cattle-grid (Watch for this with care)	Bellever
O	1.1	Turn sharp left at T junction	No sign
	.1	Bellever Forest Trail down to right. Car Park and toilets	
	.2	Over Bellever Bridge. Remains of Clapper Bridge on right	
		Total mileage on this map: 15.8	

CROWN COPYRIGHT RESERVED

On Route

Fernworthy Reservoir
An attractive and normally quiet moorland road takes us to Fernworthy. The shores of the reservoir are fenced off, but there are walks up through the trees, and above Fernworthy Forest, just over a mile to the W.S.W of our road, are the Grey Wethers Stone Circles. These are Bronze Age in origin and there are a number of Barrows close by.

Grimspound
(Turn sharp left at Point L, after ½ mile, turn sharp right, drive just over 1 mile, and then walk up path to left, opposite Headland Warren Farm.)

This is Dartmoor's best preserved Bronze Age settlement, and consists of the ruins of 24 huts in a walled enclosure with a paved entrance still visible; all in an exposed moorland setting. This provides us with the clearest possible impression of what life in Bronze Age times must have been like . . . nasty, brutish, and almost certainly short. However do not be deterred from making this most interesting visit.

Bennett's Cross
A crude medieval cross, which probably served the double purpose of marking the route across the moor from Chagford to Tavistock, and one of the boundaries of the Headland Warren, one of several medieval warrens, or game reserves.

Warren House Inn
Stands about 1,400 feet above sea level and derives its name from the Headland Warren (see above). It is now much developed, with holiday makers in mind, and is complete with 'coffee lounge'.

Vitifer Tin Mine
Not far from the Warren House Inn, and on the opposite side of the road, a path leads down to the valley of the West Webburn stream, where there are the remains of the Vitifer Tin Mine. Here will be found the artificial ravines created by the miners who worked this method in the days before shaft mining.

Postbridge
Small tourist centre in the heart of the moors with a famous 'clapper bridge', the largest on Dartmoor. This was probably built in the 13th century, for the use of pack horses travelling from the tin mines to the stannary towns of Tavistock and Chagford.

To the right of B3212 about 2½ miles to the south-west (go straight ahead at Point N) there are the remains of a gunpowder factory (behind Powder Mills Farm), which operated between 1844 and 1890. The mortar beside the track was for 'proving' the flashing qualities of the powder.

Bellever Forest Trail
This trail through the coniferous Bellever Forest is organised by the Forestry Commission, and is open to the public all the year.

Bellever Bridge (See Page 25)

1. Hut Circle, Fernworthy

2. Grimspound

3. Warren House Inn

4. Postbridge

Map 12

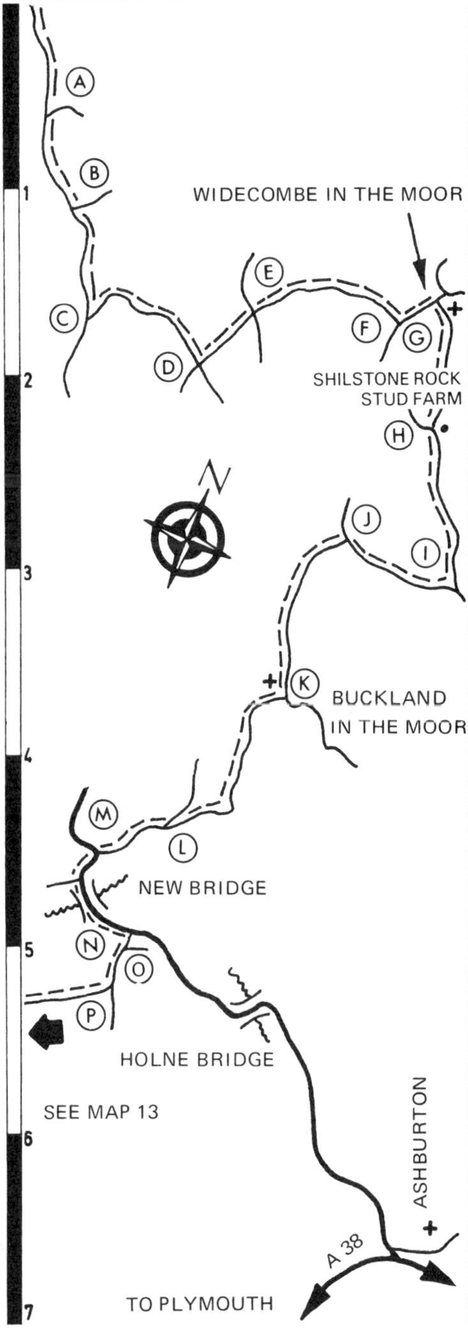

Ref	kms/Miles	Directions	Sign-posted
A	1.7	Straight, not left	Ashburton
B	.6	Straight, not left	No sign
C	.6	Turn very sharp left at Y junction (WATCH FOR THIS WITH GREAT CARE)	No sign
D	1.0	Turn left at X rds. by old cross	No sign
E	.4	Over X rds. with care, on to moorland	No sign
	.6	Start to descend steep hill	
F	.4	Turn left at T junction, at Southcombe	Widecombe
G	.3	Arrive at Widecombe, and . . .	
		Turn right immediately BEFORE church (WATCH FOR THIS WITH CARE)	No sign
	.5	Higher Venton Farm on right	
H	.3	Turn left at T junction by Shilstone Rocks Stud Farm	No sign
	.1	Climb steep hill	
I	.9	Turn very sharp right	No sign
J	.7	Turn left at T junction	Buckland
	.9	Buckland in the Moor entry signed	
K	.1	Turn right immediately beyond church. (Do not be deterred by gate-posts)	No sign
	.3	Down steep hill through splendid woods	
	.7	Over bridge crossing the River Webburn	
L	.2	Straight, not right	No sign
		River Dart now on our left	
M	.5	Turn left on brow of hill with care, on to wider road	Ashburton
	.3	Over New Bridge crossing the Dart	
N	.5	Turn right, off wider road (But keep straight on if you wish to link with Map 1, Point A at Ashburton)	Holne
O	.1	Straight, not left	Holne
P	.2	Bear right at T junction	Holne
		Total mileage on this map: 11.9	

CROWN COPYRIGHT RESERVED

On Route

Holne
Small village situated high above Buckfastleigh, with the moors less than a mile to the west and great woodlands clothing the slopes of the Dart valley to the north and east. It has a pleasant little hotel, The Church House Inn, and a small church with a beautiful early 16th century pulpit and a screen of the same period. Charles Kingsley was born here in 1819.

Venford Reservoir
Sheltering beneath Holne Moor, this rather severe stretch of water supplies Paignton, some 15 miles away to the east.

Hexworthy
Has an impressive bridge over the West Dart, with a large central arch and two smaller ones. The river here is most attractive, with a few trees relieving its overwise bare moorland setting. The Forest Inn is a favourite with anglers and pony trekkers.

Dartmeet . . . Badger's Holt
Here the East and West Dart rivers meet up after short moorland journeys, and start their beautifully wooded descent through the deep valley to Buckfastleigh. There are fine walks up the moorland valleys, or down the Dart and across to Venford Reservoir (see above). There is a welcoming cafe with large free car park, a fine road bridge and the remains of a 'clapper bridge'.

Two Bridges
A hamlet which grew up on the miners' road from Chagford to Tavistock, and now the major moorland route centre, with roads running outwards to Moretonhampstead, Tavistock, Plymouth and Ashburton. To the left of the road, about half a mile out on the Moretonhampstead road is Crockern Tor, where the "Tinners' Parliament" met to enact the Laws of the Stannaries. There is a National Park Information Centre at Two Bridges during the summer months.

Wistman's Wood
Lies about two miles up the valley of the West Dart, above Two Bridges. It is the outstanding example of three copses, all that remain of Dartmoor's native oak woodlands. This is best visited in spring, but if doing so at any time, please respect the enclosure notices of the Nature Conservancy.

The Devonport Leat
This was a channel cut into the hillside in 1794 – 95 to supply Devonport Dockyard, and drew its waters from the West Dart a little way above Wistman's Wood (see above). The channel may be traced down the west side of the Dart valley from Wistman's Wood (see also Fox Tor Mires, Page 29).

1. Combestone Tor

2. Hexworthy Bridge

3. Dartmeet, near Badger's Holt

4. Two Bridges

Map 14

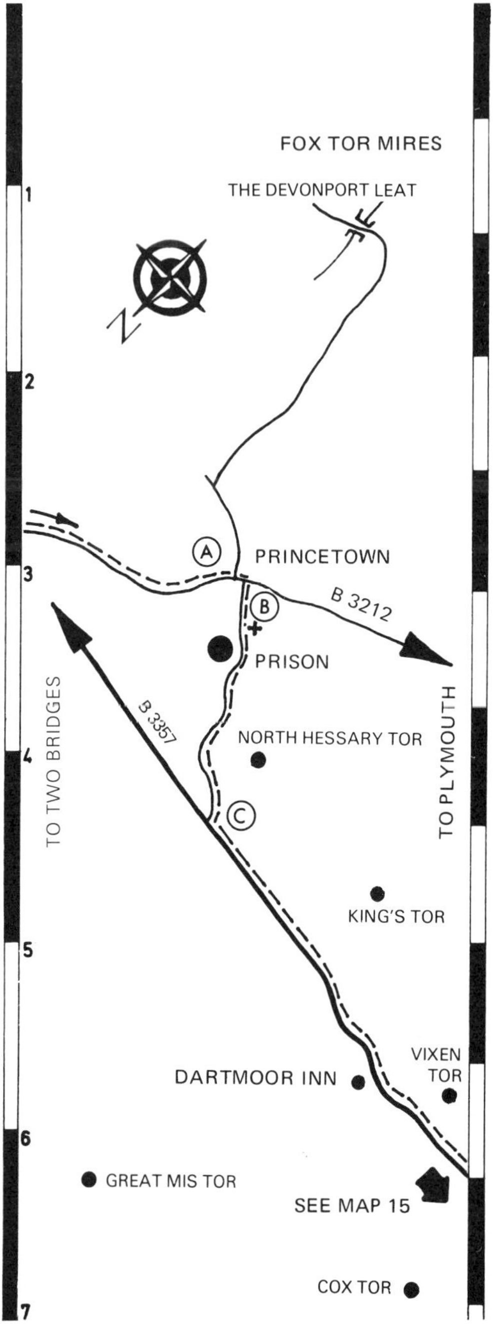

Directions — **Sign-posted**

Ref	Miles	Directions	Sign-posted
	1.1	Princetown entry signed	
A	.3	Straight, not left	No sign
		(But to explore southwards to Fox Tor Mires . . . about 3 miles . . . turn left by Methodist Chapel, and turn sharp right after ½ mile)	
B	.1	Turn right in Princetown centre	Tavistock
	.5	Prison on right	
C	.9	Fork left on to B3357 beyond cattle-grid	Tavistock
	.2	King's Tor on left	
	1.6	Dartmoor Inn on right	
	.4	Vixen Tor on left	
		Total mileage on this map: 5.1	

CROWN COPYRIGHT RESERVED

On Route

The Road to Fox Tor Mires

This diversion (see Route Details) takes us nearly three miles over quiet moorland, to the site of a disused mine. Shortly before arriving at the end of the road we cross the Devonport Leat (see Page 27) as it winds its way around the contour. There are splendid moorland views out over Fox Tor Mires, and travelling along this road one has a hint of what motoring was like before the crowds came to Dartmoor.

1. *The Devonport Leat near Fox Tor Mires*

Princetown

This grim little granite town owes its existence to the enterprise of Sir Thomas Tyrwhitt, Lord Warden of the Stannaries, and friend of the Prince Regent. Between 1785 and 1798 he built himself a mansion, Tor Royal (to the left of the road about ½ mile along the Fox Tor Mires Diversion), and with wealth obtained from his granite quarries, built many of the moorland roads in use today.

With French prisoners of war overflowing the prisons and prison hulks of Plymouth, he proposed that a prison be built on the moors to house them (they were also to prove useful for working his quarries). With land granted from the Duchy of Cornwall, by the Prince Regent (hence Princetown) the prison was built in 1806. Although closed at the end of the Napoleonic Wars (1816), Princetown Prison was opened again in 1850 for long term convicts, and although long overdue for closure, it is still in use today.

2. *Princetown Church*

With its dark grey granite, its prison, its radio and television masts, Princetown has little to offer us. We have no time for the visitor that hopes to catch glimpses of prisoners, and would urge you to pass quickly by in search of happier objectives. Please do not encourage ponies on the road by feeding them, either here or anywhere else on Dartmoor.

3. *'On the Western Fringes'*

Merrivale

This undistinguished hamlet with its bridge over the Walkham, grew up around its granite quarries, and includes the well known Dartmoor Inn, which now looks a warmly hospitable place, in marked contrast to its often bleak surroundings. From the road near Merrivale may be spotted some of Dartmoor's finest tors . . . to the right, Great Mis Tor, and Great Staple Tor, to the left King's Tor and Vixen Tor.

Bronze Age Hut Settlements abound in this area (see the 1:50,000 Ordnance Survey Map), but avoid straying too far to the right of the road, unless you are sure that the military training area is not in use.

4. *Ponies near Sampford Spiney*

Map 15

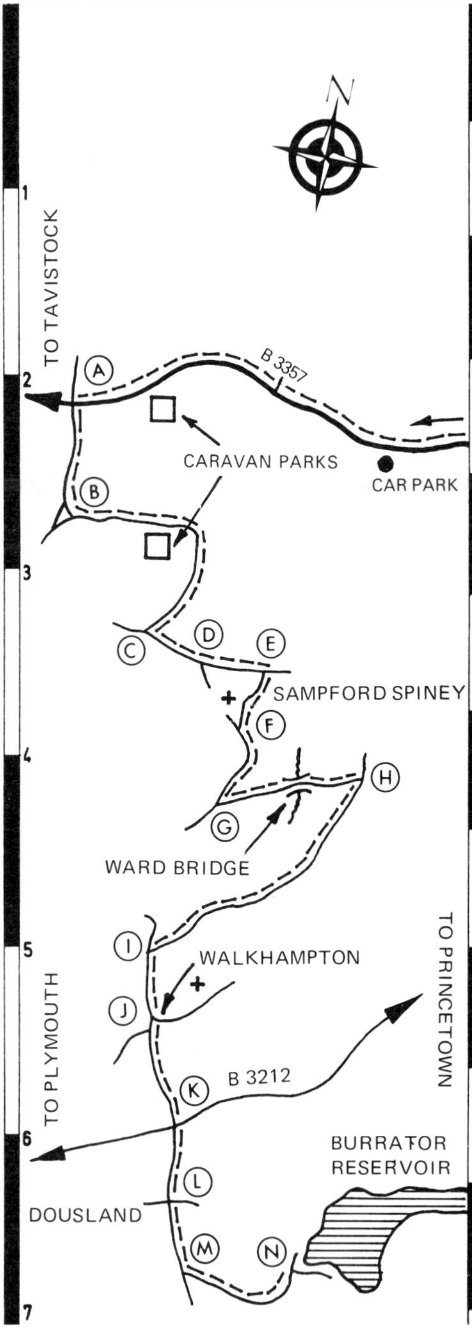

	kms Ref. Miles	Directions	Sign-posted
	.8	Good car park on left (see opposite)	
	.5	Straight not right	No sign
	.5	Caravan Park on left	
A	.3	Turn left at X rds., off B3357	Whitchurch
	.4	Cross stream at Pennycomequick	
B	.2	Fork left at T junction	Moortown
	.1	Bear left at T junction	No sign
	.5	Langstone Manor Camping and Caravan Park on right	
C	.9	Turn sharp left	Sampford Spiney
D	.5	Straight, not right	No sign
E	.3	Turn right at T junction	No sign
	.3	Sampford Spiney church on right	
F	.1	Straight, not right	No sign
G	.5	Turn sharp left	Ward Bridge
	.6	Over Ward Bridge	
H	.3	Turn **very** sharp right at top of hill (Take this very slowly. Go across and reverse to left a little, if necessary)	Walkhampton
	.4	Through attractive wood with stream	
I	1.3	Bear left at T junction	Walkhampton
J	.4	Straight, not left, beyond entry to Walkhampton, and . . .	
	.1	Fork left by village cross	Dousland
K	.6	Over B3212 with great care, by the Burrator Inn	Burrator
L	.4	Over small X rds., in Dousland hamlet	Burrator
M	.3	Fork left	Burrator
N	.8	Arrive Burrator Reservoir and link with MAP 8, POINT G	
		Total mileage on this map: 11.5	

CROWN COPYRIGHT RESERVED

On Route

Sampford Spiney
Scattered parish with a small granite church tucked away below the edge of the moors. The church has a minute south porch and although the interior has been scraped and pointed by over-enthusiastic restorers, it has an unexpected warmth of atmosphere. There is fine granite arcading, and a 15th century font in a miniature north transept. When we called here late one June evening the churchyard was still bright with flowers, and the high moorland so recently crossed already seemed far away.

1. *Our Road near Sampford Spiney*

Ward Bridge
Early 19th century stone bridge spanning the lovely Walkham river, and overlooked by wooded valley slopes. The Walkham valley from Merrivale (see page 29), down past Ward Bridge to medieval Huckworthy Bridge is attractively wooded and provides good walking. To walk up the valley to Merrivale, turn left, off the public road at Point H, walk up the track to Davy Farm, and on path beyond (about 2½ miles to Merrivale).

Walkhampton
The church, with its handsome slender tower is a landmark for miles around, and stands close to the moorland edge, well away from the village. However its interior is not really interesting enough to justify a diversion from our route. The village itself is also not exceptional.

2. *At Ward Bridge*

Burrator Reservoir
This 150-acre reservoir is claimed by many guide books to be the most beautiful in Devon. We think Tottiford (see *South Devon by Car*) even lovelier, but Burrator has a fine bowl-like setting, backed by woods and moorland, with several tors on the skyline above. There is no access to the shore, but there are fine walking possibilities up through the woods and on to the moor.

3. *Burrator Reservoir*

The Stannary Towns . . . A Note
There appears to be no doubt that Dartmoor was Europe's richest source of tin at least during the 12th century, and although the Cornish mines outstripped them in later years, the miners of Dartmoor were powerful enough to be almost outside the rule of normal law for several centuries (see Lydford, page 11, and Two Bridges, page 27). However all output had to pass through the 'Stannary Towns' of Ashburton, Chagford, Tavistock and later Plympton, and here the tin would be weighed, stamped and taxed.

4. *Road above Burrator*

INDEX

	Page
Aish	18
Ashburton	3
Avon Dam	21
Bacon, John	15
Badger's Holt	27
Baring-Gould, The Rev.	11
Becka Falls	3
Bedford, Earls and Dukes of	13
Bennett's Cross	23
Bellever Bridge	25
Bellever Forest Trail	23
Bellmaine, Robert	17
Belstone	7
Berrydown	7
Bickleigh	15
Blessed Sacrament Chapel	21
Boasley Cross	8
Bodmin Moor	13
Bowerman's Nose	5
Bovey, North	5
Bovey, River	5
Bradley Down	10
Brannoc, St.	19
Bratton Clovelly	11
Brentor	13
Brisworthy	17
Brooke Family	17
Buckfast Abbey	21
Buckfastleigh	21
Buckland Abbey	15
Buckland-in-the-Moor	25
Buckland Monachorum	15
Buckland Woods	25
Burrator Reservoir	17, 31
Cadover Bridge	17
Castle Drogo	9
Cawsand Beacon	7
Chagford	5
Cheston	18
Chudleigh, Elizabeth	19
Combestone Tor	26
Corndon Cross	22
Cornwood	17
Cranmere Pool	9
Crockern Tor	27
Dartmeet	27
Dartmoor Inn	29
Dartmoor Wildlife Park	17
Dart, River	9, 21, 25
Dart Valley	21, 27
Dart Valley Railway	21
Davy Farm	31
Devonport Leat	27, 29
Dewerstone, The	15
Dousland	30
Drake Aisle	15
Drake, Sir Francis	15
Drake Manor Inn	15
Drewsteignton	9
Drewston	4
Dunning, John	3
East Dart River	27
East Webburn Valley	25
Elford, Elizabeth	17
Erme Valley	19
Fernworthy Forest	23
Fernworthy Reservoir	23

	Page
Finch Foundry Museum	7
Fingle Bridge	9
Forestry Commission	23
Forest Inn	27
Fox Tor Mires	29
Gidleigh	7
Gidley Bridge	20
Glanville, John	13
Godolphin, Sidney	5
Great Mis Tor	29
Great Staple Tor	29
Grenofen	12
Grenville, Sir Richard	15
Grey Wethers Stone Circle	23
Grimspound	23
Hall Farm	19
Harford	19
Harold, King	7
Haytor Rocks	3
Headland Warren	23
Headland Warren Farm	23
Heathfield, Lord	15
Hembury Castle	21
Hembury Woods	21
Henry VIII	21
Hexworthy	27
Hollow Tor	2
Holne	21, 27
Holne Bridge	21, 25
Holne Chase	25
Holne Moor	27
Horrabridge	15
Hound Tor	5
Huckworthy Bridge	31
Ivybridge	18
Jurston	22
King's Tor	29
Kingsley, Charles	27
Kingston, Duchess of	19
Lady Modford's School	15
Langstone Manor	30
Lew, River	11
Lewtrenchard	11
Lobb Hill Cross	10
Lydford	11
Lydford Castle	11
Lydford Gorge	11
Manaton	5
Marchant's Cross	17
Meavy	17
Meldon Reservoir	9
Merrivale	29, 31
Moortown	6
Moretonhampstead	5
Morewellham Quay	13
Museum of Dartmoor Life	9
Museum of Rural Industry	7
National Park Information Office	27
New Bridge	25
North Bovey	5
Okehampton	9
Okehampton Castle	9
Owley	19
Paignton	27
Parke Rare Breeds Farm	3
Pennycomequick	30
Pil Tor	2

	Page
Plymouth	15
Plym, River	17
Plym Valley	15
Postbridge	23
Powder Mills Farm	23
Prideaux, John	19
Prince Regent	29
Princetown	29
Princetown Prison	29
Quarr Abbey	15
Rajah Brooke	17
Ripon Tor	2
River Dart Country Park	21
Roborough Down	15
Rushlade	2
Sampford Spiney	31
Scorhill Stone Circle	7
Shaugh Bridge	15
Shaugh Prior	15
Sheepstor	17
Sheeps Tor	17
Shipley Bridge	21
Spurrell's Cross	19
Sticklepath	7
Stannaries, The	11, 27, 31
Street, G. E.	3
Tamar Valley	13
Tavy Estuary	15
Tavy, River	9, 13
Tavistock	13
Tavistock Abbey	13
Taw, River	9
Teign, River	5, 9
'Tinner's Parliament'	27
Top Tor	2
Tor Hamlet	14
Tor Royal	29
Totnes	21
Tottiford Reservoir	31
Throwleigh	7
Throwleigh Moor	7
Two Bridges	27
Tyrwhitt, Sir Thomas	29
Ugborough	19
Venford Reservoir	27
Vitifer Tin Mine	23
Vixen Tor	29
Walkham, River	15, 29, 31
Walkhampton	31
Ward Bridge	31
Warren House Inn	23
Webburn, River	25
Weet, Great	4
West Dart River	27
West Okement River	9
West Webburn River	23
Whitchurch	13
White Lady Waterfall	11
Williams, Mary	11
Williams, Thomas	19
Widecombe Fair	25
Widecombe-in-the-Moor	25
Wistman's Wood	27
Wyddon, Sir John	7
Yarner Wood National Nature Reserve	3